MEET THE FUSCO BROTHERS!

MEET THE FUSCO BROTHERS!

by J.C. Duffy

Andrews and McMeel
A Universal Press Syndicate Company
Kansas City • New York

The Fusco Brothers is distributed by Universal Press Syndicate.

Meet The Fusco Brothers! © 1990 by Lew Little Enterprises, Inc. All rights reserved. Printed in the United States of America. No part of this book may be used or reproduced in any manner whatsoever without written permission except in the case of reprints in the context of reviews. For information write Andrews and McMeel, 4900 Main Street, Kansas City, Missouri 64112.

ISBN: 0-8362-1849-3

Library of Congress Catalog Card Number: 90-82678

5

OPTI-MISM: A SAD AND BEAUTI-FUL THING...

THE FUSCO BROTHERS FORM A SEMI-HUMAN CHAIN TO THE REFRIG-ERATOR:

WHEN FISHING FOR COMPLIMENTS BECOMES FISHING FOR VERIFI-CATION.... [CAUTION IS RECOMMENDED.]

EDIBLE COM-PLEX

LANCE WOULD LAUGH WHENEVER HE RECALLED HIS EMPTY EXISTENCE BEFORE GOLF...

THAT DAY IN THE PARK WHEN INNOCENT FLIRTATION LED TO NEAR TRAGEDY!

TODAY'S GAG:

"NOT PLAYING WITH A FULL DUCK."

SAY, DO YOU MIND IF WE TAKE A BREAK? I'M STARVED!!

THAT TEARS IT! WHO THE HECK IS THIS GUY TO COME IN MY HOUSE AND MAKE A FOOL OF ME?!?!

LANCE! LANCE! IT'S ONLY A COMIC STRIP! CALM DOWN!!

YOU'RE RIGHT... I'M SORRY!

BONUS GAG

HEADACHE?

NO THANKS, I'VE ALREADY GOT ONE....

AL HAS AN OUT-OF-DRAWING EXPERIENCE!

HELP!

GOSH! YOU DON'T SEE THIS KIND OF THING IN "BEETLE BAILEY"!

WITH GOOD REASON, PERHAPS!

SATURDAY NIGHT FEEBLE!!

SATURDAY NIGHT, AND THE JUNGLE IS ALIVE WITH ANCIENT PRIMAL SOUNDS....

HEAVEN MUST BE MISSING AN ANGEL....

HELLO, MURIEL? IT'S RÖLF....RÖLF FUSCO.... YES, FROM THE.... HELLO? HELLO? HELLO??

HI! YOLANDA? IT'S RÖLF, SWEETIE. I WAS JUST....HELLO? HELLO!! OPERATOR!!

CAMILLE? HI! THIS IS RÖLF FUSCO.....YES! IT HAS BEEN QUITE A WHILE....OH, REALLY? NO KIDDING....WELL, CONGRATULATIONS...

SATURDAY NIGHT, AND THE JUNGLE IS ALIVE WITH ANCIENT PRIMAL SOUNDS....

COOSH!

ERP.

CAGNEY! LACEY! GET IN HERE!

8

A NOTE ARRIVES UNDER THE DOOR, AND RÖLF KNOWS THAT UNTIL HE READS IT, IT COULD BE ANYTHING....

DEAR RÖLF,
YOU DO NOT KNOW ME, BUT PERHAPS YOU KNOW MY WORK. I SAW YOU IN THE PET SHOP AND SIMPLY HAD TO MEET YOU. I'LL BE AT THE PINKY LEE MONUMENT AT 8:30.
SINCERELY,
CATHERINE DENEUVE
XXXXOOOO

DEAR MR. FUSCO,
YOU KNOW THAT 10 MILLION DOLLARS I'M ALWAYS TALKING ABOUT ON TV? WELL, GUESS WHAT! IT'S YOURS, PAL!
YOUR PAL,
ED McMAHON
P.S. CHECK ENCLOSED.

SIRS:
YOU KEPT US AWAKE UNTIL DAWN WITH YET ANOTHER OF YOUR CRAZED HOOTENANNIES. ANOTHER SUCH ERUPTION AND THE F.B.I. WILL BE NOTIFIED.
STERNLY,
YOUR NEIGHBORS
P.S. SOME PEOPLE HAVE TO WORK FOR A LIVING!

....SOMETIMES THERE IS SIMPLY NO HURRY ON THESE THINGS.

AH, CATHERINE, YOU IMPETUOUS THING!!

Getting A Sandwich Hot...

MICROWAVE (3 MINUTES)

DING!

GOSH, WHAT AN AGE WE LIVE IN!!

HYPNOSIS (5½ HOURS)

YOU ARE GROWING WARM.... WARMER.....HOT!! YOU FEEL YOU SHALL GO MAD!!

DON JOHNSON-LOOK (20 SECONDS)

HI, THERE...

FOR GALS ONLY!!

FAB KISSABLE CLOSE-UP OF LARS FUSCO!!

LARS LUVS:

PLACE YOUR PICTURE HERE.

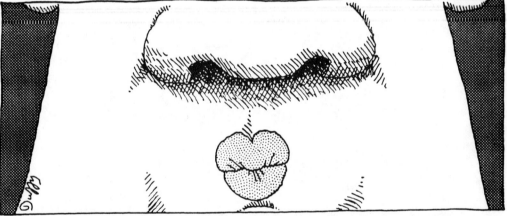

NOTHIN' SAYS LOVIN' LIKE SOMETHIN' FROM THE CLOSET...

HAPPY BIRTHDAY, EMO, TO MY FAVE-RAVE NEPHEW!

I'M YOUR ONLY NEPHEW, UNCLE LANCE.

QUIBBLE, QUIBBLE! OPEN UP!!

REALLY, YOU SHOULDN'T HAVE!

TRUE.

SAY....SAY...SAY!! AREN'T THESE THE SKATES I GAVE YOU FOR KWAANZA?

DON'T WORRY, THEY'LL ADJUST....AND SO WILL YOU.

CONVERSE K TAYLOR 14/EEEE

THAT HELPS.... THANKS...

AND THE SKATE KEY SHOULD TURN UP REAL SOON!!

WAH!! UNCA RÖLF!!!

THE DAY AXEL REALIZED HE WAS ADOPTED.

(BY A FAMILY WITH A SMALL STREAK OF CRUELTY.)

LANCE AND GLORIA'S FAVORITE TIME TO BREAK UP WAS DURING BREAKFAST.

4 HEADACHES FROM HELL!

I'D LIKE YOU TO READ THIS ARTICLE, LANCE.

CLICK

"HOW TO GET YOUR MAN TO CUDDLE MORE"?

RIGHT.

YOU AND YOUR WOMEN'S MAGAZINES.... HOW COME MY MAGAZINES NEVER HAVE ARTICLES LIKE "HOW TO GET YOUR WOMAN TO CUDDLE LESS"?

THEY DON'T RUN ARTICLES LIKE THAT IN TV GUIDE.

CLICK

WHY CAN'T I SLEEP? AFTER AN EMOTIONALLY DRAINING DAY IN FRONT OF THE TV, I SHOULD BE EXHAUSTED....

WHAT TIME IS IT? 4 O'CLOCK!! I NEED SOME REST!!

MAYBE I SHOULD HAVE SOME WARM MILK? NAH.... EXERCISE? I THINK NOT.... A MIDNIGHT SNACK? HMMM....

I CAN'T WAIT THAT LONG.... MAYBE THESE AFTERNOON NAPS AREN'T WORKING.

WHAT THE.... WHAT AM I EATING HERE?

LOW-CHOLESTEROL EGG SUBSTITUTES.

FAKE EGGS? I'M EATING FAKE EGGS? MY BODY IS A DELICATE MECHANISM - NOT TO MENTION A TEMPLE!

I REFUSE TO PUT MYSTERY MATTER INTO MY TEMPLE!!

WHERE DO THEY GET FAKE EGGS?

FROM FAKE CHICKENS.

OKAY THEN.

Panel 1: AH, SUMMERTIME IN NEWARK! I HATE TO LEAVE IT, LANCE!

FORCE YOURSELF... ANYWAY, WE'RE ONLY GOING TO PARAMUS— WE'LL BE BACK IN TIME FOR "GERALDO", DON'T WORRY....

Panel 2: GEE, THIS IS JUST LIKE "ROUTE 66"- 2 YOUNG, HANDSOME GUYS, CRUISING THE LAND, LOOKING FOR ADVENTURE.... ROMANCE.....

ODD JOBS....

WELL, MAYBE WE CAN SKIP THE ODD JOBS....

Panel 3: ....OR MAYBE "EASY RIDER" ....2 LOVEABLE MISFITS, IN SEARCH OF AMERICA .... AND GIRLS!!

I THINK THEY GET THEIR HEADS BLOWN OFF AT THE END OF THAT ONE....

Panel 4: HOW ABOUT AN ABC-AFTER-SCHOOL SPECIAL CALLED "THE FUSCO BROTHERS SCHLEP TO PARAMUS TO BORROW RENT MONEY FROM UNCLE WALTER"??OKAY?? IS THAT ALRIGHT, MR. BRINGDOWN??? MR. REALITY?!!??

Panel 5: NOTHING PERSONAL, RÖLF— EVERYBODY NEEDS A HOBBY—MINE JUST HAPPENS TO BE STEPPING ON PEOPLE'S DREAMS....

RÖLF FUSCO WITNESSES THE **INVASION OF THE JUNE TAYLOR ROACHES!**

YOIKS!!!

CLICK

...TWO, THREE, KICK!!

Panel: BEFORE HIGH TECHNOLOGY, IT WOULD SOMETIMES TAKE A WOMAN'S FRIENDS <u>WEEKS</u> TO CONVINCE HER TO STOP SEEING AL FUSCO....

AND YOUR EYES....HOW THEY SHIMMER! LIKE THE SUN GLISTENING OFF THE BACKS OF SEALS CAUGHT IN AN OIL-SPILL....AND THEN THERE ARE YOUR EARS....

HELLO? IS SOMEONE THERE WITH YOU??

IT'S JUST THE TV....GO ON.

WHAT A JERK!

AMAZING.

DUMP HIM.

IS HE CUTE?

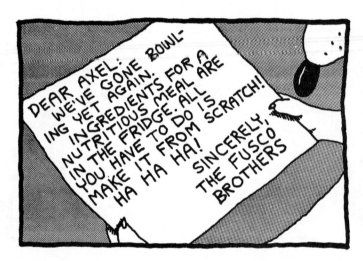

BRIEF ENCOUNTER

A FINE PILSNER LAGER, WITH A HINT OF LIME.... VERY GOOD, SIR. I'M FEELING FESTIVE.

COULD I TROUBLE YOU FOR A LIGHT, HANDSOME STRANGER? SORRY, FRESH OUT.

HANDSOME STRANGER? SHE DIDN'T WANT A LIGHT, YOU OAF! WHERE'S THE OLD SNAPPY COMEBACK?

PARDONNEZ-MOI, OH VIRILE SPECIMEN, BUT DO YOU HAVE THE TIME? SORRY, I PAWNED MY WATCH A FEW DAYS AGO.

EXCELLENT. THANK YOU.

RÖLF AND AXEL SPEND ANOTHER CONSTRUCTIVE AFTERNOON WATCHING "WHEEL OF FORTUNE"....

WHAT DO YOU THINK IT SAYS?

"EYES IN THE BACK OF MY HEAD".... IT'S OBVIOUS.

IT COULD SAY "EWES IN THE BACK OF MY HERD"...

IF WE LIVED ON A SHEEP RANCH, THAT MIGHT BE A NORMAL GUESS....AS IT IS, I RECOMMEND YEARS OF THERAPY.

YES, I SUPPOSE I WAS PREOCCUPIED WITH IT AT THE TIME....THAT WAS IN GRADE SCHOOL.... PLEASE CONTINUE....

BY HIGH SCHOOL I GUESS YOU COULD SAY I WAS OBSESSED....BUT IN A HEALTHY KIND OF WAY, I'D SAY.... PLEASE CONTINUE....

THEN, IN COLLEGE.... PLEASE CONTINUE.... ZZZZZZ....

WRONG NUMBER FROM HELL!

SOMEWHERE IN NEWARK, A WELL-MEANING WOMAN ATTEMPTS PHONING HER FAVORITE YARN EMPORIUM...

KNITWIT... KNITWIT... KNITWIT... ...AH, HERE WE GO!

MEANWHILE, ACROSS TOWN, LANCE FUSCO IS MINDING HIS OWN BUSINESS...

WHOA!

RING! RING!

BUT **FATE** REQUIRES THAT THE YARNLESS GAL MIS-DIAL..... A HUMAN MISTAKE....

HELLEW?

HELLO, IS THIS THE KNITWIT?

UNFORTUNATELY FOR LANCE, HIS CLEVER REJOINDER OCCURS TO HIM AFTER HANGING UP....

OH YEAH!?!?

EDITORIAL

AS MANY OF YOU MAY KNOW, A LOT OF SUCCESSFUL SYNDICATED CARTOONISTS DON'T DRAW THEIR STRIPS AFTER THEY GET BIG....

THEY PAY OTHER, STRUGGLING ARTISTS TO DRAW THEM....

STILL OTHERS DON'T EVEN WRITE THEM—MAYBE THEY BLACKMAIL GHOSTWRITERS INTO WRITING THEM, USING, LET'S SAY, POLAROIDS THEY'D LIKE KEPT QUIET, FOR INSTANCE....

WELL, YOU'LL BE HAPPY TO KNOW THAT **THE FUSCO BROTHERS** ARE BOTH WRITTEN AND DRAWN AS PART OF A PRISON PAROLE INCENTIVE PROGRAM.

THANK YOU.

AL · LARS · ROLF · LANCE · AXEL

QUITE AN IMPRESSIVE COLLECTION OF LP's, LOUISE.

THANKS, LARS.

IT'S NOT REALLY MY MAIN MUSICAL FORMAT AT THIS POINT, THOUGH....

MINE EITHER.

AN EVENING WITH PINKY LEE

IT ISN'T EASY KEEPING UP WITH THE LATEST TECHNOLOGY....

OH, I KNOW! WHAT DO YOU HAVE—CD's?

78's.

I'M LOOKING FOR SOMETHING IN AN "I'M-SORRY" PRESENT.

WHAT WOULD A BIG LUG LIKE YOU HAVE TO BE SORRY ABOUT?

YOU'D BE SURPRISED....APPARENTLY.

WELL, HOW ABOUT SOMETHING IN PEARLS?

I'M NOT THAT SORRY.

HOW SORRY ARE YOU?

HMMM.... MAYBE "SORRY" ISN'T THE RIGHT WORD....

ACTUALLY, I GUESS I'M LOOKING FOR MORE OF A "TOO-BAD-YOU-MISUNDERSTOOD ME" PRESENT....OR MAYBE A "HOW-UNFORTUNATE-YOU-DON'T-APPRE-CIATE-ME-FOR-WHO-I-AM" GIFT....

HAVE YOU LOOKED IN CRACKERJACKS?

WHERE'S THAT?

RIGHT NEXT TO PEANUTS, POP-CORN, AND PRETZELS.

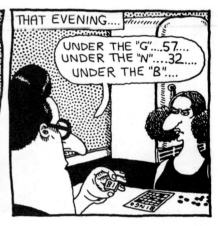

23

LIFE AMONG THE SO-CIALLY IN-EPT.

DEAR GLORIA, HOW CAN I EVER THANK YOU FOR YOUR KIND GIFT? HOW COULD I EVER THANK YOU ENOUGH?

ACTUALLY, I COULD NEVER THANK YOU ENOUGH....WAS THAT THE GENERAL IDEA? AH, NOW I BEGIN TO SEE!!

DO YOU JUST WANT ME TO FEEL BAD, OR WHAT?? WELL, I WON'T STOOP TO YOUR LEVEL, BABY!!!

YEAH!!

I REFUSE TO GET CAUGHT UP IN YOUR SICK LITTLE GENEROSITY GAME!!! BITTERLY LANCE FUSCO

YOU CAN'T BE TOO CAREFUL WITH A CUNNING WOMAN.

THE DAY AL FUSCO WENT A LITTLE TOO FAR WITH HIS HOBBY, PHILOSOPHY, AND BECAME.... **TRAPPED IN A TILTED UNIVERSE!!!**

[NOSTALGIA.]

DINNERTIME, AL....WHENEVER YOU'RE QUITE THROUGH....

IT'S FROM THE LANDLORD. HE WANTS THE RENT.... I THINK HE MEANS IT.

WHAT? IT'S ONLY OCTOBER 4TH AND HE'S SENDING US THREATENING LETTERS?

MAN! THAT REALLY STEAMS ME! WHATEVER HAPPENED TO PATIENCE? WHATEVER HAPPENED TO HUMAN COMPASSION? WHATEVER HAPPENED TO THE SIXTIES?? FOUR LOUSY DAYS LATE, AND THIS GUY IS THREATENING PEOPLE!! AND UPSETTING AN INNOCENT DOG!!!

WOLVERINE.

WHATEVER!!

ACTUALLY, HE'S ONLY ASKING FOR JULY'S RENT.

I'LL SEE WHAT WE'VE GOT...

ASK DR. SCIENCE.

"IS YOUR HAIRLINE RECEDING?"

"NO, IT'S NOT, BUT THANK YOU SO MUCH FOR ASKING."

"HMMM....IT LOOKS HIGHER, SOMEHOW...."

"THAT'S BECAUSE, IN A CHILLY ROOM, LIKE THIS ONE, THE PLASTIC IN MY GLASSES CONTRACTS, AND IT GIVES THAT ILLUSION...."

"OH...."

"IT'S THE SAME SCIENTIFIC PHENOMENON THAT HAPPENS TO THE ELASTIC IN YOUR UNDERWEAR."

"HEY, DO YOU WANT TO CLOSE THE DOOR?"

"NOT ESPECIALLY, MAN..."

"HOW MANY TIMES HAVE I TOLD YOU NOT TO DROP YOUR BOOKS ALL OVER THE FLOOR?"

"I CAN'T SAY I RECALL THE EXACT NUMBER, RÖLF.... ....I'D HAVE TO LOOK IT UP."

"IT MUST BE THE SCHOOL PLAY HE'S REHEARSING.... I GUESS HE'S STUCK IN CHARACTER."

"WHAT THE HECK ARE THEY DOING— "BLACKBOARD JUNGLE"??"

"WHO WANTS TO GO AROUND ACTING LIKE JULIE ANDREWS FOR TWO WEEKS...."

THE SOUND OF MUSIC

"DINNER IS SERVED!"

"WHAT'S THIS— PICK-UP-STICKS?"

"YOU'VE HEARD OF HAVING YOUR PASTA "AL DENTE", OR FIRM?"

"YES...."

"WELL, THIS IS HAVING IT "AL FUSCO", OR RAW."

"WHERE ARE YOU GOING?"

"I'M GOING "ALFRESCO", OR OUTDOORS."

THE SCRAB-BLE FIEND!

HMMMM....

THERE...."FLADISH"....14 POINTS, PLUS 50 POINTS FOR USING ALL MY LETTERS.

IN YOUR MIND, MAYBE. USE IT IN A SENTENCE.

WELL, I CAN'T REALLY USE IT IN MIXED COMPANY....

I CHALLENGE.

OH, ALRIGHT! LET'S SEE...."SHE REMOVED THE SILKEN KIMONO FROM HER SHOULDERS AND IT FELL BELOW HER FLADISH."

I CHALLENGE!

ACTUALLY, IT'S MORE OF AN ABSTRACT CONCEPT THAT YOU CAN'T REALLY USE IN A SENTENCE.

I CHALLENGE!!

WELL, THAT WOULD BE FINE, BUT I LENT THE GOOD DICTIONARY TO THE LONELY CHILD DOWN THE STREET WITH THE SERIOUS ILLNESS....

SOME PEOPLE CAN'T DEAL WITH LOSS GRACIOUSLY.

SLAM!

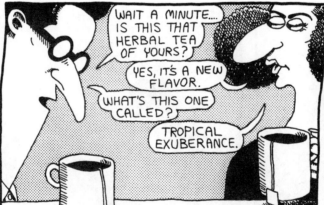

29

STILL STINGING FROM A NASTY SERIES OF REJECTIONS, AL DECIDES TO TAKE THE CAUTIOUS APPROACH FOR A FEW YEARS....

IS THIS SEAT TAKEN?

HELP YOURSELF.

AXEL, I WONDER IF YOU COULD HELP OUT WITH A PROBLEM....

POSSIBLY.

I JUST GOT THIS FREE PHONE FOR SUBSCRIBING TO THAT SWIMSUIT ISSUE....

YOU MEAN THE ONE WHERE THEY KEEP SENDING YOU ALL THOSE SPORTS MAGAZINES YOU DON'T WANT?

THAT'S THE ONE....

SO WHAT'S THE PROBLEM?

WELL, THE PHONE CAN BE PROGRAMMED TO DIAL UP TO NINE "FREQUENTLY-CALLED NUMBERS"... BUT I WANT EVERYBODY TO BE ABLE TO USE IT....

AND YOU DON'T KNOW HOW TO FAIRLY DIVIDE UP THE NUMBERS?

NO, BETWEEN THE FOUR OF US, WE COULD ONLY COME UP WITH THREE NUMBERS:...WE WERE HOPING YOU COULD ROUND IT OUT WITH ANOTHER SIX....

WHAT HAPPENED?!!? THAT LOOKS LIKE LANCE!!!

NEAR AS WE CAN FIGURE IT, THE BULB BURNED OUT IN THE FRIDGE, AND HE BIT INTO THIS QUICHE THINKING IT IT WAS A BURRITO....

...HE MUST HAVE GONE INTO SHOCK....

THE PARAMEDICS ARE WITH HIM NOW....

33

DING!

IF YOU CAN READ THIS, YOU'RE TOO CLOSE.

CAUGHT TAILGATING ON THE HIGHWAY OF LOVE.... HOW EMBARRASSING.

LANCE! WHAT DO YOU THINK?

I'M AFRAID TO THINK, AL....

I THOUGHT, THIS HALLOWEEN, INSTEAD OF JUST COLLECTING STUFF FOR ME, ME, ME, I'D ALSO COLLECT SOME MONEY FOR A WORTHY CAUSE....YOU KNOW— "TRICK-OR-TREAT FOR UNISEX!"

PLEASE GIVE

I BELIEVE THAT'S "TRICK-OR-TREAT FOR UNICEF!"....

I'LL BE RIGHT BACK...

WHAT'S THE ZIPCODE AROUND HERE, LANCE?

ZIPCODE? LET'S SEE....ZIPCODE... THERE'S A 5 IN THERE.... TOWARD THE END....

WHAT DO YOU NEED IT FOR?

I'M SENDING FOR A FREE CATALOGUE.

FOR WHAT?

FARM MACHINERY.

WHY?

WHY? BECAUSE IT MIGHT BE NICE TO GET SOME MAIL! SOMETHING FOR ME! SOMETHING I CAN CALL MY OWN!!

THIS HAS BEEN A VERY MOVING EXPERIENCE....TO PROVE IT, I'LL BE MOVING TO ANOTHER ROOM NOW....

AL FUSCO, MR. INTER-NATIONAL, DEMONSTRATES *"Dining Around The World"*....

HOLLYWOOD....

CHECK!

LONDON....

CHEQUE!

PRAGUE....

CZECH!

NEXT LESSON: 10 TRANSLATIONS OF "I SEEM TO HAVE LEFT MY WALLET IN MY OTHER SUIT."

YOU'RE LATE. IS A FINE WINE LATE BECAUSE IT TAKES AWHILE TO REACH PERFECTION?

WHY DON'T YOU HAVE A SEAT AND FIGURE OUT WHAT YOU'D LIKE TO DO TONIGHT WHILE I TURN THAT OVER IN THE PRIVACY OF MY BRAIN....

OKAY....

I THOUGHT MAYBE WE COULD STAY IN AND WA—

HMMM?

MENU

TAXI!!

DINNER AND DANCING....WHAT A LOVELY IDEA!!

LOVELY IDEAS ARE MY HOBBY.

THE FUSCO BROTHERS RENT A SECLUDED BEACH HOUSE IN ORDER TO STARE OUT AT THE SEA AND CONTEMPLATE THE MEANING OF LIFE....

NOT EVERYONE IS AS SUPPORTIVE AS HE MIGHT BE....

MEANING, SCHMEANING! I'M GOING INTO TOWN!!

35

OKAY, BEFORE WE START OUT, ARE ALL SEAT BELTS BUCKLED?

YEP.

YEAH.

FULL TANK OF GAS?

YES.

TIRE PRESSURE OKAY?

AL, DON'T BE SUCH A NERVOUS NELLY.

WHAT ABOUT FLARES?

FLARES??? AL, WE'RE GOING TO THE 7-ELEVEN! WE'LL BE BACK IN 5 MINUTES!

DO YOU WANT A SLURPEE?

I CAN'T....I'M THE DESIGNATED DRIVER.

LANCE, WHILE YOU'RE UP, HOW ABOUT A BACKRUB?

NO THANKS....

I COULD USE ONE AFTER I SIT DOWN, THOUGH....

I'LL BE RIGHT OUT....I'M JUST SLICING UP SOME OF THIS CHEESE YOU HAD IN THE FRIDGE....

DON'T BRING THE KNIFE.

WHAT'S SO FUNNY?

THIS OLD DIARY.... ISN'T IT AMAZING, THE STUPID THINGS WE COME UP WITH?

TALK ABOUT EMBARRASSING! AM I BLUSHING? WHAT GARBAGE!

WE ALL GO THROUGH IT....

NOT LIKE THIS! MAN, WHAT TRASH!!

OH, DON'T BE SO HARD ON YOURSELF....

ME?? THIS IS YOURS, PAL! I WOULD NEVER BE DUMB ENOUGH TO LEAVE SOMETHING LIKE THIS HIDDEN UNDER A BUNCH OF SOCKS!!

MY DIARY

WHOOMPH!

IT'S FROM THE LANDLORD....HE WANTS THE RENT.

HE'S GOT SOME COLOSSAL NERVE!

I KNOW.

DID HE EVER FIX THAT LEAKING FAUCET?

ACTUALLY, YES, HE DID.

HOW ABOUT THE GARBAGE DISPOSAL?

WE DON'T HAVE A GARBAGE DISPOSAL.

OH.

WHAT ABOUT THE BROKEN LOCK?

UMM....YES, COME TO THINK OF IT.

HMMM....THAT'S DIFFERENT. MAYBE IT'S TIME WE WENT TO WORK.

IT'S ONLY RIGHT.

OKAY, YOU LOOSEN THE FAUCET, I'LL BREAK THE LOCK.

RIGHT.

OKAY, WHAT CAN YOU TELL ME ABOUT IZMIR?

IZMIR? HMMM....

CITY IN WESTERN TURKEY....

WESTERN TURKEY....UMMM....

? ? ? ?

THE ANCIENT SMYRNA....

THE ANCIENT SMYRNA? YOU USED TO GO OUT WITH HER, DIDN'T YOU LARS?

THAT WAS MYRNA, AND SHE WAS ONLY FIVE YEARS OLDER THAN ME....

THAT'S WHAT I MEAN....

THANKS A LOT! NOW HOW AM I SUPPOSED TO PASS GEOGRAPHY, GRADUATE, AND GO ON TO BE A PRODUCTIVE MEMBER OF SOCIETY?

THAT SOUNDS MORE LIKE A SOCIOLOGY QUESTION.... ASK RÖLF.

WHOSE TURN IS IT TO TAKE OUT THE TRASH?

I DID IT LAST WEEK.

NO, I DID IT LAST WEEK!!!

YOU KNOW, THERE ARE ENOUGH OF US HERE THAT SOMEBODY COULD GET AWAY WITH ONLY CLAIMING HE DID IT TWO WEEKS AGO....

I DID IT TWO WEEKS AGO.

RÖLF TRIES THE "SENSITIVE POET" APPROACH, AND HIS MASTERPIECE, "PAIN!", SOON HAS THE CHICKS FIRMLY IN HIS GRIP....

OUCH! OH, MAN! YOWIE!! OOH!! PAIN!!!

TAKE TWO ASPIRIN!!

TO AL FUSCO, "HINT" IS JUST A FOUR-LETTER WORD....

HI, LINDA? THIS IS AL FUSCO....

YOU SAID I SHOULD CALL BEFORE STOPPING OVER....

WELL, I'M CALLING.... WHAT'S THAT?

I SHOULD WRITE BEFORE CALLING??

WHAT'S THE ZIP CODE OVER THERE...?

HELLO?

HELLO!

OPERATOR!

YOU KNOW, LANCE, YOU LOOK LIKE KIRK DOUGLAS WHEN YOU'RE ANGRY....

REALLY? KIRK DOUGLAS? GEE.... THANKS.... SUDDENLY I'M NO LONGER ANGRY....

OF COURSE, I DON'T HAVE A CLEFT CHIN....

YOU DON'T HAVE A CHIN. I'M ANGRY AGAIN.

DID I SAY KIRK DOUGLAS? I MEANT MIKE DOUGLAS.

SOME INDIVIDUALS JUST CAN'T TAKE A COMPLIMENT....

YOU KNOW, AXEL, YOU'RE REALLY VERY MATURE FOR A 15-YEAR-OLD.

ACTUALLY, I'M 16, AND THESE ARE THE COMICS.

WELL, FOR A DOG....

WOLVERINE.

DO YOU WANT ANYTHING FROM THE STORE?

41

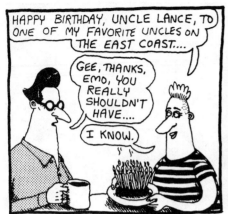

42

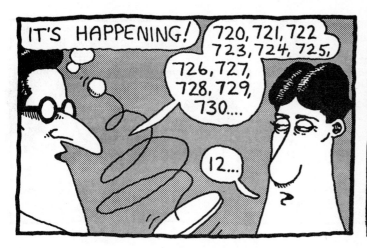

43

YOU CAN DRESS THEM UP, BUT YOU CAN'T TAKE THEM ANY WHERE...

SUNDAY MAIL? EITHER I'M IN POSTAL HEAVEN, OR ROD SERLING IS OUTSIDE INTRODUCING "THE TWILIGHT ZONE"!

HEY! IT'S MY CREDIT CARD FROM SCHLÜRMAN'S DEPARTMENT STORE!

THAT'S NICE.

HEY! MY CREDIT LIMIT IS ONLY 300 DOLLARS! THEY GAVE YOU 500 DOLLARS, AND YOU'RE A BUM!!

THAT'S SHOW BIZ.

WHAT DOES THAT MEAN??

THAT'S THE WAY THE COOKIE CRUMBLES...THAT'S THE WAY THE BALL BOUNCES... THAT'S SHOW BIZ.

THAT'S NOT SHOW BIZ! YOU'RE A MAN, AND I'M A WOMAN!!

I DOUBT THAT.

YOU DOUBT THAT?!?!

YOU KNOW WHAT I MEAN.

UH-OH! I THINK I HEARD ABOUT THIS ON "GERALDO"!!

WHAT A LOVELY DINNER, LARS! I HAD NO IDEA YOU COULD COOK!

THERE'S A LOT YOU DON'T KNOW ABOUT ME, NATALIE.

LIKE WHAT?

LIKE WHAT?

FOR INSTANCE....

FOR INSTANCE?

SUCH AS....

SUCH AS?

I THINK IF I LEARNED ONE MORE FASCINATING THING ABOUT YOU, WHY, I DON'T KNOW WHAT I'D DO!!

I'M AN ASTRONAUT.

AXEL FUSCO, CEREAL KILLER!

IS THAT THE LAST OF THE COUNT CHOCULA?? I HAD MY HEART SET ON THAT!!

SO?

SO? SIMPLY PUT, THERE COULD BE BLOODSHED.

WHAT DO YOU MEAN?

TAKE THE "L" OUT OF "AXEL", AND IT'S "AXE".... THINK ABOUT IT!!!

BOY, YOU REALLY DON'T KNOW SOMEBODY TILL YOU LIVE WITH THEM!!

I CAN'T TALK RIGHT NOW, AXEL, I'M INVOLVED IN THE GAME.

MAYBE THERE'S ANOTHER GAME YOU SHOULD GET INVOLVED IN, AL.....

WHAT GAME IS THAT?

THE GAME OF LIFE.

LIFE? LIFE'S OKAY....

I LIKE THE PICTURES.... IT'S NEWSWEEK THAT GIVES ME A HEADACHE.

AL FUSCO, "MR. INTER-NATIONAL", INSISTS ON DOING SANTA WITH A FRENCH TWIST....

HEAU-HEAU-HEAU!!

WHEECH WAY TO ZEE MEELK AND ZEE COOKEEZ?

LET HIM EAT CAKE!

DEAR UNCLE WALTER, THANKS FOR THE CHRISTMAS GIFT. I AM ENCLOSING IT HEREWITH.

THE RETRACTABLE LEASH, WAS, I'M SURE, INTENDED AS A HUMOROUS PRELUDE TO YOUR REAL GIFT.

IT GAVE ME ME QUITE A LAUGH.

I AM RETURNING IT SO THAT YOU MAY RE-USE IT AS A HUMOROUS PRELUDE AGAIN AND AGAIN, AND WE CAN LAUGH ABOUT IT FOR YEARS TO COME.

GRATEFULLY YOURS, Axel

P.S. FEDERAL EXPRESS IS OPEN UNTIL 8 O'CLOCK.

AW! IS LANCE POUTING? DID GLORIA HURT HIS FEELINGS??

YES, ACTUALLY.

REALLY? GEE, I'M SORRY....I WAS JUST KIDDING....YOU'RE SO SENSITIVE SOMETIMES....

WHILE AT OTHERS....

YOU MUST THINK I HAVE A PRETTY THICK HIDE....

I DON'T KNOW— I WISH I'D BROUGHT MY CALIPERS.

DID YOU EVER CONSIDER ATTACHING THE TV TO THE CEILING, LANCE? EASIER ON THE NECK....

THE LANDLORD SAID NO.

AREN'T YOU AFRAID THAT IF YOU LIE THERE LONG ENOUGH, YOU'LL OSSIFY?

YOU'VE HEARD OF OVERACHIEVERS? PEOPLE WHO TRY TO COMPENSATE FOR THEIR INADEQUACIES BY OVERDOING? WELL I'M AN UNDERACHIEVER....IT'S DESIGNED TO DISTRACT PEOPLE FROM MY UNFAIR ABUNDANCE OF GIFTS.

IT'S WORKING.

LIFE IN THE FUSCO LANE....

BRUNCH TUESDAY? LET ME CHECK MY BOOK....

IMPOSSIBLE. I'M TIED UP UNTIL TWO....WHAT ABOUT A LATE POWER LUNCH?

FABULOUS! LOVE YA, BABE!

JUST REMIND ME TO GET HOME BY FOUR...."GERALDO" LOOKS PRETTY DARN SIZZLING!!

PRACTICING FOR NEW YEAR'S EVE, LANCE?

CRANKA-CRANKA-CRANKA!

NO, AL, THIS IS A FEZ I'M WEARING....I'VE JOINED A BIZARRE CULT IN WHICH WE ALL CRANK THESE NOISE-MAKERS TO THE TUNE OF "HEARTBREAK HOTEL", TO SUMMON THE GHOST OF ELVIS....

OH....WELL, YOU BE CAREFUL, NOW—THOSE CULTS CAN BE DANGEROUS!

I WILL.

WELL, RÖLF, HERE IT IS, ANOTHER DECADE....

YEP.

JUST WHEN YOU THINK YOU'RE GETTING THE HANG OF ONE, THEY SPRING ANOTHER ONE ON YOU....

MY ONLY QUESTION IS, NOW THAT I'VE FINALLY ADJUSTED TO THE SEVENTIES, SHOULD I GO DIRECTLY TO THE NINETIES, OR WORK ON THE EIGHTIES FOR MY OWN PERSONAL GROWTH?

THAT'S A TOUGH ONE, AL.

LANCE! YOU DECIDED TO PLAY BALL AFTER ALL! I REALLY APPRECIATE THIS! HOW ABOUT GOING OUT FOR A LONG ONE?

I'LL GO YOU ONE BETTER—HOW ABOUT IF I GO OUT FOR A LONG, TALL COLD ONE?

BUS

THIS WOULD NEVER HAPPEN IN "THE FAMILY CIRCUS."

WHAT ABOUT DOING SOMETHING LATER.... BOWLING? ROLLER DERBY? TAFFY-PULL? OPERA? HOOTENANNY? PINOCHLE? WHATEVER YOU WANT.... YOU NAME IT!

WHY ARE YOU BEING SO ACCOMMODATING, LANCE?

I WAS JUST WATCHING "OPRAH".... SHE DID A WHOLE SHOW ON "JERK BOYFRIENDS"....

DID YOU SEE IT?

I WAS THE WOMAN BEHIND THE SCREEN WITH THE ELECTRONICALLY ALTERED VOICE.

NICE RING.... WHAT IS IT?

BLACK ONYX.

OH, A MOOD RING.

I SAID IT'S BLACK.

THAT'S WHAT I MEAN.

IT NEVER CHANGES.

EXACTLY.

NOBODY LIKES A SMART-ALEC DOG.

WOLVER-INE

ANYWAY, MAXINE, ARE YOU BUSY TONIGHT?

YOU'RE STAYING IN TO WASH SOME UNMENTIONABLES?

LIKE WHAT??

I KNOW THAT'S WHY THEY CALL THEM UN-MENTIONABLES....

YOU CAN TELL ME....I'M A DOCTOR.

OKAY, SO I'M NOT A DOC-TOR....I'M A PRIEST....ALL RIGHT, I'M NOT A PRIEST.... I'M A SCIENTIST....

HELLO??

HELLO?!!?

WHERE TO, YOU ASK? WELL, WE'RE FOUR YOUNG, FOOTLOOSE, VERY ATTRACTIVE MEN, IN A CAB IN ONE OF THE MOST EXCITING CITIES ON EARTH-NEWARK, NEW JERSEY....WHAT DO YOU SUGGEST?

I SUGGEST YOU SOMEHOW TRY TO FIND YOUR WAY BACK TO REALITY, AND FRANKLY, I DON'T KNOW IF I CAN DRIVE YOU THERE, PAL.

AL FUSCO, MAN OF A MILLION MOODS....

GEE, I FEEL GREAT! IT'S SO GOOD TO BE ALIVE!....TO BE ME!! ....TO BE AL FUSCO.!!!

KNOW WHAT I MEAN?

NOT REALLY.... I'VE NEVER *BEEN* AL FUSCO.

SUDDENLY, AL IS OVERCOME BY A LETHAL DOSE OF PHILOSOPHY, HIS HOBBY....

GEE, MAYBE *I'VE* NEVER REALLY BEEN AL FUSCO, EITHER....

THAT'S DEEP, AL.

ARE YOU OKAY, AL?

HUH?

OH....YEAH....I WAS JUST THINKING ABOUT THAT OLD QUESTION, "IS THE CUP HALF-FULL, OR HALF-EMPTY?"....AS YOU MAY KNOW, PHILOSOPHY IS MY HOBBY....

I KNOW.... WELL?

I'VE DECIDED IT'S NONE OF MY MY BUSINESS.

THAT'S SO DEEP, I'M GETTING THE BENDS.....IF YOU WANT ME, I'LL BE IN THE DECOMPRESSION CHAMBER.

WHAT DO YOU THINK ABOUT A SOUFFLÉ FOR DINNER?

TOO WIMPY.

WHAT ABOUT STEAK FLAMBÉ?

NOTHING WITH AN ACCENT OVER THE "E"....

HOW ABOUT A QUICHE WITH A MANLY FILLING?

IT WOULD HAVE TO BE PRETTY MANLY.

BRAUNSCHWEIGER.... EXTRA BRAUN, HOLD THE SCHWEIGER.

THAT COULD WORK.

ECONO-DOG FOOD ONCE AGAIN....WHY DO I TAKE IT?

AXEL

WHAT AM I— A MAN OR A MOUSE? A DOG OR A WOLVERINE? GOOD QUESTIONS, ACTUALLY....

AM I A WIMP? SPINELESS? MADE OF JELLO?!!?

WHAT FLAVOR...?

OBVIOUSLY, I'M HUNGRY....I'LL WORRY ABOUT THE IMPLICATIONS LATER....

AXEL

P

THE FAMILY THAT JOKES TOGETHER, PROVOKES TOGETHER....

NEW SHIRT?

NO THANKS, I JUST BOUGHT ONE....

I REALIZE THAT'S AN OLD JOKE....

THAT'S OKAY, YOU'RE AN OLD MAN.

WAS THERE ANYTHING ELSE?

I JUST REALIZED WHERE I'VE SEEN THAT SHIRT BEFORE....

GQ?

HEE HAW.

GEE, THERE'S NOTHING MUCH ON TV TONIGHT....

TV

I COULD REALLY GO FOR A GOOD MATCH OF LADIES' MUD-WRESTLING RIGHT ABOUT NOW....

YOU PROBABLY DIDN'T MEAN TO SAY THAT....

I'M ASSUMING YOU'D LIKE TO AMEND THAT STATEMENT....

YOU'RE RIGHT, I'M VERY SORRY....

I MEANT WOMEN'S MUD-WRESTLING.

I'D LIKE TO APPROVE YOUR LOAN, MR. FUSCO, BUT YOU'LL HAVE TO BE MORE SPECIFIC ABOUT EMPLOYMENT.

OKAY....REMEMBER HOW OZZIE NELSON NEVER SEEMED TO GO TO WORK ON "OZZIE AND HARRIET"? THAT'S BECAUSE HIS JOB WAS BEING OZZIE NELSON ON THE SHOW....MY JOB IS BEING LANCE FUSCO.... GET IT?

NOT REALLY....

TURN AROUND.

OH, MY GOD!! IT'S ALLEN FUNT!!

YOU KNOW, LANCE, A WOMAN NEVER KNOWS IF A MAN IS INTERESTED IN HER MIND OR HER BODY....NO MATTER WHAT HE TELLS HER....

I UNDERSTAND....IT SOUNDS LIKE A TOUGH LEGACY.

IT IS! WOMEN HAVE A LOT OF TOUGH LEGACIES!

I SYMPATHIZE....IN FACT, THAT'S THE FIRST THING I NOTICED ABOUT YOU....

WHAT DO YOU MEAN?

I'VE ALWAYS BEEN A LEGACY MAN.

YOU'RE SO SENSITIVE.

THANKS.

OOH, MAN! I MUST BE GETTING OLD! ALL THESE ACHES AND PAINS....

WELL, AL, IT STILL BEATS THE ALTERNATIVE.

CRUNCH!

PSYCHOLOGY TOMORROW

WOW! YOU'RE RIGHT! I NEVER THOUGHT OF IT THAT WAY! THANKS FOR THE HEALTHY DOSE OF PERSPECTIVE, LANCE!!

YOU'RE WELCOME.

I COULD BE WALKING AROUND SMELLING LIKE BEN-GAY!!

RIGHT....

LANCE, I THINK WE'RE HAVING TROUBLE WITH LANGUAGING.... IT'S SO IMPORTANT IN COMMUNICATION.

LANGUISHING? SPEAKING FOR MYSELF, I THINK I EXCEL AT LANGUISHING.

THAT'S VERY TRUE....NO, I SAID LANGUAGING.

LANGUAGING?? I'M SO FAR FROM GOOD LANGUAGING, I'VE NEVER EVEN HEARD OF IT! IS THAT FROM ONE OF YOUR GOOFY NEW AGE RELATIONSHIP MANUALS?

I HEARD IT ON TV.

LET ME GUESS— OPRAH? PHIL? GERALDO? SALLY JESSY? DR. RUTH?

DRAGNET.

FRIDAY NIGHT AND YOU'RE HOME HANGING PICTURES, AL?

SINCE THE PHONE WASN'T EXACTLY RINGING OFF THE HOOK, I THOUGHT AT LEAST I'D USE MY TIME CONSTRUCTIVELY....

THEN AXEL KNOCKED MY CAN OF YOO-HOO INTO THE TOOLBOX, AND NOW EVERYTHING'S ALL STICKY!!

RING! RING!

HELLO? TAMMY?? NO, I'M NOT BUSY—I WAS JUST WAITING FOR MY NAILS TO DRY!!

HELLO??

HELLO?!!?

BLOOD IS THICKER THAN WATER, AND POSSIBLY MAYONNAISE....

WHAT ABOUT A DRIVE-IN? WE COULD TURN THE SOUND DOWN!

DON'T BE JUVENILE, AL.

THAT WAS COMPARATIVELY MATURE, BETTY, TAKE MY WORD.

I BELIEVE AL PROBABLY MEANT THAT ARTY, FOREIGN FILMS— HIS FAVORITE— HAVE SUBTITLES ANYWAY, AND DON'T REALLY REQUIRE SOUND.... RIGHT, AL?

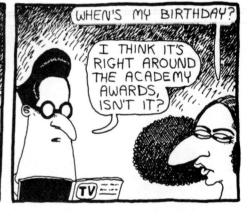

WOULD YOU LIKE TO RIDE IN THE CART, AXEL?

LANCE, I'M 16 YEARS OLD, CHRONOLOGICALLY, AND EMOTIONALLY I COULD BE YOUR GRANDFATHER....

NO, I DON'T WANT TO RIDE IN THE CART!

GEE, I'M SORRY, I KEEP FORGETTING WHAT A MATURE YOUNG MAN YOU REALLY ARE....IT MUST BE THE BABY FACE... HOW ABOUT IF I MAKE IT UP TO YOU WITH A BIG BOX OF DOGGIE BISCUITS?

YOU'RE REALLY CRUISIN' FOR A BRUISIN', PAL.

I LOVE THESE COZY LITTLE FRENCH JOINTS, DON'T YOU?

YES, BUT WHEN I COME TO THEM, I GET HOME SICK.

REALLY? I THOUGHT YOU WERE BORN AND RAISED HERE IN NEWARK, LARS.

I WAS....

WHEN I COME HERE, I GET REMINDED OF THAT....

THEN, WHEN I GET HOME, I'M SICK.

WHAT THE HECK IS THAT?

IT'S A WHITE PICKET FENCE....I'M TRYING TO GIVE THE ILLUSION OF BEING A NORMAL AMERICAN FAMILY.

BUT WE DON'T EVEN HAVE A LAWN!

I'VE GOT SOME ASTROTURF IN THE STATION WAGON.

WHAT STATION WAGON??

I WAS GOING TO MENTION THAT.

HOW WOULD YOU LIKE YOUR EGGS TODAY, LANCE?

HOW WOULD I LIKE THEM? I'D LIKE THEM IN PARIS, FRANCE, INSTEAD OF NEWARK, NEW JERSEY, THAT'S HOW I'D LIKE THEM TODAY.

WELL, YOU'D HAVE TO ASK FOR "OEUFS" THEN, NOT EGGS....

I COULD LIVE WITH THAT HARDSHIP, AL.... BUT THANK YOU VERY MUCH, MR. INTERNATIONAL.

WHAT'S HAPPENING ON TV?

IT'S AN ORVILLE REDENBACHER POPCORN COMMERCIAL.

IS HIS GRANDSON GARY IN IT?

YES.

WHY THE BIG INTEREST?

I LIKE THE IDEA THAT THIS OLD GOOFY GUY IS GOING TO PASS ON THE TORCH TO HIS GOOFY GRANDSON....AT THIS RATE, THE WORLD MAY BE IN FOR CENTURIES OF GOOFY POPCORN COMMERCIALS....

I'M GLAD YOU CAN FIND COMFORT IN THAT....

NOW, IF ONLY GERALDO AND OPRAH WOULD HAVE A CHILD....

IS IT OKAY TO HAVE THE BUSINESSMAN'S LUNCH IF I'M NOT A BUSINESSMAN?

YES.

OKAY....AND SOME WON TON SOUP.

I'LL HAVE THE FUN LO PING.

SORRY, NO FUN TILL 4 O'CLOCK.

THE STORY OF MY LIFE....OKAY, NEVER MIND THE FUN.....I DON'T NEED FUN.... I'VE HAD PLENTY OF FUN IN MY LIFE ALREADY....

JUST BRING ME A GLASS OF WATER AND THE CHECK.

I'D LIKE AN EXTRA-LARGE PIZZA WITH ONE-FIFTH ANCHOVIES, ONE-FIFTH PEPPERONI, ONE-FIFTH....WHAT'S THAT? YOU DON'T DIVIDE YOUR PIZZAS INTO FIFTHS? I DIDN'T THINK SO, BUT I'M NOT IN CHARGE AROUND HERE....

OKAY, I'LL CALL YOU BACK IF THERE'S A BREAKTHROUGH AT THE BARGAINING TABLE, THOUGH FRANKLY, THE SMELL OF COMPROMISE IS NOT IN THE AIR....

AND HOW CAN WE HELP YOU TODAY?

GEE, I DUNNO.... THEY ALL LOOK SO FRIENDLY... SORT OF....

MAYBE I'LL GO WITH THIS GUY HERE.... I JUST MIGHT DEVELOP A LOVE-HAKE RE-LATIONSHIP....

HAKE

BUDDY, I'VE HEARD EVERY FISH PUN ON EARTH, SO I'M PRETTY JADED....AT THIS POINT I ONLY TOLERATE SCROD JOKES.... COME BACK WHEN YOU HAVE A GOOD ONE.

AW....WHAT A CUTE LITTLE GUY!! HOW OLD IS HE?

SIXTEEN.

BUS

IS THAT DOG-YEARS, OR PEOPLE-YEARS?

DON'T GET ME STARTED, LADY!

67

OK, LANCE, IT'S FEBRUARY....ARE YOU READY TO MOVE MY AIR CONDITIONER DOWN TO THE BASEMENT YET?

ALMOST.

WHAT DOES THAT MEAN?

IT MEANS THAT, POSSIBLY, AFTER A SERIES OF NEGOTIATIONS, OFFERS AND COUNTERPROPOSALS, WE MAY BE ABLE TO DO BUSINESS.

YOU CAN'T DO BUSINESS WITH HITLER.

DON'T YOU THINK THAT'S A LITTLE SEVERE?

OK... MUSSOLINI.

THAT'S BETTER.

INEZ? HI! IT'S RÖLF FUSCO....

I'VE GOT ONE CRACKED CRAB AND ONE SLIGHTLY NUTTY LOBSTER OVER HERE...

WHAT DO YOU SAY YOU COME ON OVER, AND THE FOUR OF US TRY A LITTLE PRIMAL SCREAM THERAPY.... HELLO? HELLO?

BOY, NOT MUCH OF A SENSE OF HUMOR FOR A PSYCHIATRIC EMERGENCY ROOM NURSE, I MUST SAY...

HOW COME I NEVER MEET ANY WOMEN IN HERE? SOME BEAUTY WANTING TO BORROW MY FABRIC SOFTENER ... NOT THAT I HAVE ANY....

NO SNEAKERS IN THE MACHINES, PAL.

HUH? WHO ARE YOU?

I'M THE OLD GUY WHO'S ALWAYS WATCHING "WHEEL OF FORTUNE" IN THE CORNER.... I'M THE MANAGER.

OH ...OK.

THIS IS NOT EXACTLY WHAT I HAD IN MIND....

BY THE WAY, WOMEN CAN BUY FABRIC SOFTENER IN THE MACHINES, SO DON'T GET ANY FUNNY IDEAS ...

Row 1

WINTER IN NEWARK....

STOP

SIDEWALK CAFÉS NO LONGER BUBBLE WITH CHAMPAGNE AND LAUGHTER....

GARÇON?

GONE ARE THE WARM BREEZES... THE BARE MIDRIFFS....THE DIMPLED KNEES....

BUT A MAN MUST HAVE ROOTS.... LOYALTY....STABILITY....A PLACE TO CALL HOME....

WHEN IT'S WINTER IN NEWARK.

TAXI

WHERE TO, PAL?

TAHITI!

Row 2

AL FUSCO: PARTY ANIMAL, PATRIOT OR DUNCE?

I'M HOME, GUYS!

AL? ARE YOU JUST GETTING IN?

IT'S 8 IN THE MORNING!

YOU KNOW HOW CRAZY THESE LINCOLN'S BIRTHDAY PARTIES CAN GET!!

RIGHT....

I'M STILL RECOVERING FROM FLAG DAY....

Row 3

THE VALENTINE GENIUS....

BOING!

HEART-SHAPED TOAST? WHAT'S THE OCCASION?

MUST BE A FLAWED LOAF.

HEY-THE EGGS ARE SHAPED LIKE NEW JERSEY! IS THAT A HINT?

SCRAMBLED EGGS ARE ALWAYS SHAPED LIKE NEW JERSEY, LANCE.

I JUST GET THE FEELING YOU'RE TRYING TO TELL ME SOMETHING, GLORIA....

WORK ON IT, SHERLOCK.

71

HEADING FOR THE LAST ROUND-RUMP....

IS THIS FRESH?

IS THE POPE SWEDISH?

KID, YOU'LL FIND THAT MIXING HUMOR WITH DEAD ANIMAL FLESH CAN DRIVE SOME MEN TO RASH ACTS....

SOMEDAY YOU MAY THANK ME FOR THIS VALUABLE INFORMATION.

SLAM!!

YOW!!

OK, I THINK I'M READY....DON'T MOVE.

I'VE BEEN HOLDING THIS PHONY FROZEN SMILE FOR 5 MINUTES! I FEEL LIKE A VENTRILOQUIST!

I DON'T THINK I LIKE THE IMPLICATION....

I JUST MEANT IT'S NOT EASY TALKING WITHOUT MOVING YOUR LIPS....

I DIDN'T THINK YOU HAD LIPS.

CLICK!

DO YOU THINK THE FILM RECORDED THE EXCLAMATION POINTS ABOVE YOUR HEAD?

!!*?&#!%π!!&!!

RECORD THIS!

SNEAK PREVIEW!! DICK CLARK'S CENSORED COMIC BLOOPERS!

TAKE 1 I SAY, RÖLF, COULD YOU KASS THE PETCHUP? I MEAN— OH, DARN!

KASS THE PETCHUP?

HA-HA-HA!

TAKE 2 I SAY, RÖLF, COULD YOU....UH....COULD YOU POSSIBLY....AW, JEEZ! HA-HA-HA-HA-HA!

SPLOOSH!

HYUK! HYUK! HYUK!!

TAKE 3 I SAY, RÖLFFF!!! HO-HO-HO-HO!! HAW-HAW-HAW!! HEH-HEH-HEH-HEH!!

DON'T WORRY, THIS WILL ALL SEEM HILARIOUS ONCE DICK AND ED PUT IN THE LAUGH TRACK!

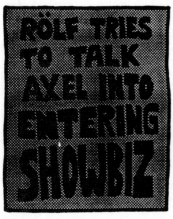

DARK NIGHT OF THE SOLE...

HERE YOU GO, BOB—A MEAL FIT FOR A KINGFISH! HA-HA-HA!

ONE OF THESE DAYS I'M BUSTIN' OUT OF THIS JOINT, AND I'M TAKIN' ONE OF YOU LOUSY SCREWS WITH ME!!

I THINK MAYBE THE TV WAS A MISTAKE, LARS....

ANOTHER CUP OF COFFEE?

I GUESS SO....

ACTUALLY, I'M JUST WAITING FOR THE RAIN TO LET UP.... I DIDN'T FEEL LIKE BUYING AN UMBRELLA OR A HAT....

WHY DON'T YOU JUST BUY A NEWSPAPER?

WHAT A TREMENDOUS IDEA!

5 MINUTES LATER....

NOW AT LEAST I'LL HAVE SOMETHING TO READ WHILE I WAIT....

RIGHT.

SMOKING FISH: SOME TRAGIC TESTIMONIALS!

I CAN STOP ANY TIME I WANT...HONEST!!

ALL MY HEROES SMOKED FISH—BOGART....DYLAN....JULIA CHILD....

EMPTYING ALL THOSE FISHTRAYS AFTER A PARTY....WHAT A HADDOCK!

I WAS TRYING TO FILL AN EMPTINESS INSIDE....SEARCHING...SEEKING....WHY DO YOU THINK THEY CALL IT FISH?

THERE WAS A LOT OF PIER PRESSURE.

78

CARE FOR A PFEFFERNUSSE?

A WHAT?

PFEFFER-NUSSE.

IT SOUNDS LIKE JUNK FOOD FOR SENIORS, OR SOMETHING....

IT MIGHT PROVIDE THAT EXTRA PEP YOU REQUIRE FOR THOSE ZANY TEEN-AGE HOOTENANNIES....

I DON'T DO HOOTE-NANNIES, BUT IF I DID, ALL I COULD MUSTER AFTER ONE OF THESE BABIES WOULD BE A MILD HOKEY-POKEY, POPS.

ONLY IN AMERICA:

Liberty and Justice for Al...

LIBERTY   AL   JUSTICE

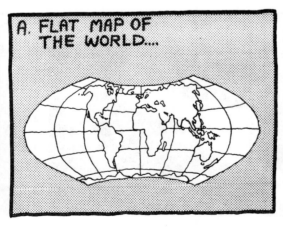

GEOG-RAPHY MADE E-Z!

A. FLAT MAP OF THE WORLD....

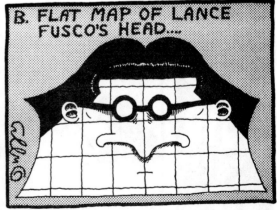

B. FLAT MAP OF LANCE FUSCO'S HEAD....

DISHEARTENED BY HIS LACK OF SUCCESS WITH WOMEN, LARS TURNED TO THE SOLACE OF **ART**....

IF ONLY ONE'S DAY-TO-DAY PROBLEMS WERE MORE ECLECTIC...

AL INSTRUCTS LANCE ON THE FINER POINTS OF CHEER-FULNESS....

WHY DO YOU ALWAYS WANT TO ARGUE, LANCE?

IT TAKES TWO TO TANGO, GLORIA.

AND THAT'S ANOTHER THING: YOU ALWAYS WANT TO GIVE ME THE BLAME!

HALF THE BLAME. THAT'S STILL TOO MUCH!!

OK, LET'S DROP IT.

POWERMONGER.

IT TAKES TWO TO POWERMONG.

WHAT'S UP, AL?

I'M HAVING MY MIDNIGHT SNACK.

BUT IT'S ONLY 7 O'CLOCK.

I WAS FEELING A LITTLE TIRED, AND I WAS AFRAID I'D SLEEP THROUGH MY ACTUAL MIDNIGHT SNACK....

BUT WE JUST FINISHED DINNER....

ACTUALLY, WHILE YOU WERE HAVING YOUR DINNER, I WAS REALLY HAVING MY LUNCH, SINCE I NAPPED THROUGH LUNCH....SO, TECHNICALLY, I'M STARVED!!

AND, CLINICALLY, YOU'RE A VERY SICK MAN.

WHAT, WITH ALL THE FUSS OVER THE LEGEND OF SAINT PATRICK DRIVING THE SNAKES OUT OF IRELAND, WE TEND TO FORGET THE LEGEND OF AL FUSCO DRIVING THE ROACHES OUT OF NEWARK....

AND STAY OUT!!

HOLLAND TUNNEL

[TOO BAD ABOUT THEM COMING BACK, OF COURSE.]

82

ALWAYS PREPARED, RÖLF WAS KNOWN AS THE

Boy Scout of Love....

THANKS FOR THE RIDE, MICHELE. WOULD YOU CARE TO COME IN FOR SOME COFFEE?

IT'S LATE....

IT WOULD KEEP ME AWAKE.

WE HAVE DECAFFEINATED.

GROUND OR INSTANT?

EITHER.

YOU PROBABLY DON'T HAVE MILK.

SURE WE DO.

I PREFER CREAM.

NO PROBLEM.

SUGAR?

YES. OR ARTIFICIAL SWEETENER.

I CAN ONLY DRINK COFFEE IN CHINAWARE.

WHICH DYNASTY?

OKAY, SO I'M NOT THE EASIEST PERSON TO GET ALONG WITH.

SO I UNDERSTAND.

THANKS FOR UNDERSTANDING, AT LEAST.

THAT'S NOT WHAT I MEANT.

MENU

WHAT COULD YOU HAVE POSSIBLY MEANT, THEN? CERTAINLY NOT SOMETHING SARCASTIC—NOT WHEN I'M SPILLING MY GUTS....

YOU CALL THAT SPILLING YOUR GUTS?

STILL GUTS RUN DEEP.

WHAT'LL IT BE?

SUDDENLY I'M NOT TOO HUNGRY.

MENU   MENU

DING DONG!

WHO IS IT?

MR. FUS-CO?

WHAT A COINCIDENCE... I, TOO, AM MR. FUSCO....

IT'S MR. FISK, OF THE I.R.S.

NO ONE IS HOME AT THE MOMENT... AT THE TONE, PLEASE LEAVE YOUR NAME AND MESSAGE....

YOU CAN'T AVOID ME FOREVER, MR. FUSCO!

KNOCK KNOCK!

BEEP!

HERE YOU GO, AXEL! IT'S THAT NAUTICAL LOOK THE LADIES GO FOR!

FORBES

CAN YOU SAY "AHOY"?

AHOY THIS, AL!

IT MIGHT BE EVEN BETTER IF YOU EMPTY THE BOWL FIRST.

I THINK I HEAR MY CAB!

AXEL

84

THAT LADDER LOOKS AWFULLY RICKETY, AXEL..

YEAH!!

MAYBE YOU SHOULD GO STEADY IT, RÖLF.

BUT LANCE IS CHANGING THE LIGHT BULB FOR YOU....

UNDER DURESS.

STILL, MAYBE YOU SHOULD GO STEADY IT....

!#?!&*%©!!

I'M TOO YOUNG TO GO STEADY.

OKAY, AXEL, I CHANGED THE LOUSY LIGHT BULB...DON'T SAY I NEVER DID ANYTHING FOR YOU.

GEE, LANCE, I FEEL ALL WARM AND RUNNY INSIDE...IT MUST HAVE FELT LIKE THIS ON WALTON'S MOUNTAIN, I BET....

GOOD NIGHT, JOHN BOY.

GOOD NIGHT, GRANDPA.

STROKE! STROKE!

STROKE? NO THANKS, BUT PERHAPS YOU'D CARE TO JOIN ME IN A HEART ATTACK....

WHAT IS THAT YOU'VE GOT ON THE STEREO, LANCE?

"ZAMFIR PLAYS YOUR PANFLUTE FAVORITES."

I SEE...PRETTY PEPPY STUFF...WHY DON'T YOU PUT ON SOME MOTOWN AND WE CAN DANCE, MAYBE....

AT MY AGE, GLORIA, MOTOWN HAS BEEN REPLACED BY MOTRIN.

LANCE, I NEED YOUR OPINION.

NATURALLY.

I'VE PAID ALL OF THE ABSOLUTELY NECESSARY BILLS FOR THE MONTH...

YEAH....

AND THERE'S ENOUGH MONEY LEFT TO PAY ONE LUXURY BILL....

PAY THE CABLE TV BILL.

IT'S PAID.

WHAT ABOUT URSULA, THE MASSEUSE?

PAID.

WHAT'S LEFT?

GAS, ELECTRIC AND RENT.

HMMM....

LANCE, I'M TIRED OF YOU SAYING YOU'RE GOING TO DO SOMETHING, AND THEN NOT DOING IT.

PERHAPS, GLORIA, YOU SHOULD LEARN FROM OUR FRIENDS, THE CONDIMENTS, AND TAKE WHAT I SAY WITH A GRAIN OF SALT....

MAYBE I'M LOOKING FOR A LOW-SODIUM RELATIONSHIP.

ALL RIGHT, TAKE IT WITH A GRAIN OF PAPRIKA.

I DON'T KNOW WHAT THAT'S SUPPOSED TO MEAN.

THAT'S THE GENERAL IDEA.

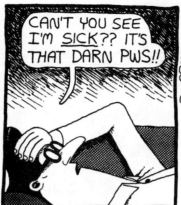

FINANCIALLY EMBARRASSED, LANCE DECIDES IT'S TIME TO PUT HIS NOSE TO THE GRINDSTONE.

DO YOU EVER GET DOWN IN THE DUMPS, AXEL?

YOU MEAN LIKE WHEN YOU'RE RIDING YOUR BIKE, AND THE USUALLY UPLIFTING "RUPPER-PUP-PUP" OF THE BALLOONS AGAINST YOUR SPOKES SOUNDS SUDDENLY HOLLOW?

UH...YEAH, I GUESS THAT'S WHAT I MEAN.

NO, I NEVER GET THAT WAY.

HI, GLORIA. HOW'S TRICKS?

OH, HI, AXEL! IT SEEMS WE NEVER SEE EACH OTHER.

YES, WELL, LANCE LIKES TO KEEP HIS WORLDS SEPARATE.

YES, WHY IS THAT?

AS A CHILD, IN THE 1850S, THE INDIANS CAPTURED RUSTY, MY BELOVED HOBBYHORSE, AND IT WASN'T UNTIL A CENTURY LATER THAT WE WERE REUNITED BY RALPH EDWARDS ON "THIS IS YOUR LIFE."...IT HAD AN EFFECT, I GUESS.

SEE YOU IN THE FALL, GLORIA.

RIGHT.

THE FAULTY JAM:

THE FUSCO BROTHERS REFORM "THE FUSSTONES", AND REALIZE THEY ARE A BIT RUSTY....

LANCE, GIVE ME AN "E".

I BELIEVE HE SAID "GIVE ME AN 'E'"... NOT "GIVE ME A KNEE"!!

OH, SORRY...I'LL HAVE THE LINGO DOWN BY THE GIG, MAN....

OOH...SHOW BIZ IS MY LIFE!!

WOULDN'T YOU KNOW IT?!!? THE SECOND TIME I TRY WATCHING THIS SHOW AND IT'S A REPEAT OF THE SAME EPISODE I WATCHED IN THE FALL!

AND IT'S A REALLY DE-PRESSING ONE!!

OH, I HATE WHEN THAT HAPPENS... WHAT SHOW IS IT, AL?

IT'S CALLED "THE CBS EVENING NEWS."

WOULD IT KILL YOU TO TAKE ME ON A LITTLE FANTASY WEEKEND, LANCE?

TAHITI

I'M DOING YOU A FAVOR, GLORIA... IT'S IMPORTANT TO HAVE FANTASIES, YET FANTASIES AREN'T MEANT TO COME TRUE... THAT'S WHY THEY CALL THEM FANTASIES, AND NOT PLANS.

GEE, YOU'RE A REGULAR WERNER AIRHEAD... WHEN DID YOU TURN INTO A NEW AGE PHILOSOPHER?

WHAT TIME IS IT NOW?

AL, DO YOU EVER THINK ABOUT MINDING YOUR WAIST?

YOU KNOW WHAT THEY SAY, AXEL—"THE WAIST IS A TERRIBLE THING TO MIND."

THAT'S "THE MIND IS A TER-RIBLE THING TO WASTE."

THAT'S ALSO BAD.

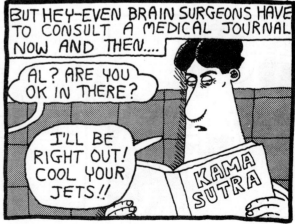

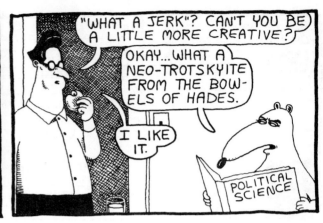

98

99

IT'S REALLY VERY SIMPLE, AL... I'M TRYING TO EXPERIENCE THE SPRINGTIME IN SECTIONS—THE SIGHTS, THE SOUNDS, THE SMELLS—THAT WAY I CAN SAVOR EVERY ASPECT OF IT... IT DOESN'T MAKE ME OUT OF MY MIND.

I GET IT—IT'S KIND OF LIKE THE WAY I EAT THE CENTER OF AN OREO COOKIE FIRST....

ACTUALLY, THAT'S NOT A BAD ANALOGY... MAYBE YOU DO GET IT....

THANKS.

MAYBE I AM OUT OF MY MIND....

IT'S FROM MA...

MA FUSCO?

THAT'S THE ONE...

SHE'S COMING FOR A VISIT.

THAT'S NICE... POSSIBLY. FOR HOW LONG?

DOESN'T SAY... SHE SAYS THAT ONCE AGAIN, PA WOULD LOVE TO COME TOO, BUT "THOSE PESKY PRISON OFFICIALS ARE SO DARN STRICT"....

DID HE SAY "MAY I?"?

APPARENTLY.

I DON'T THINK I GET THE CONCEPT, GLORIA...TWO PEOPLE WILL ALWAYS BE TWO PEOPLE... NO?

YOU DON'T WANT TO GET THE CONCEPT, LANCE...YOU'RE BLOCKING! THE IDEA OF TWO PEOPLE SO CLOSE THEY BECOME ONE... THEY BECOME MESHED!!

MESHED? YOU MEAN LIKE MESHED POTATOES?

SOMETHING LIKE THAT....

IT'S MA FUSCO, HERE FOR A VISIT! HOW ARE MY BIG BABY BOYS??

"TOP OF THE WORLD, MA!!"

JAMES CAGNEY IN "WHITE HEAT," 1949...I MADE THEM WATCH A LOT OF TV WHEN THEY WERE KIDS....

THAT EXPLAINS MUCH.

SO, MA—HOW LONG ARE YOU STAYING?

AS LONG AS MY PRESENCE HELPS MAINTAIN THE USUAL HIGH STANDARDS OF HILARITY AROUND HERE, LARS!

WHAT TIME IS THE NEXT BUS?

! ! !

SEE WHAT I MEAN?!!?

WHAT SIGHTS WOULD YOU LIKE TO SEE WHILE YOU'RE IN NEWARK, MA?

JUST SEEING MY BIG BABY BOYS IS PLENTY, AL.

WELL, WHAT WOULD YOU LIKE TO DO?

JUST CLEANING UP AFTER YOU BIG SLOBS MAKES ME HAPPY.

BUT WHAT CAN WE DO FOR YOU??

I ACCEPT CASH AND TRAVELER'S CHECKS, BUT MY CREDIT CARD REGISTER IS ON THE FRITZ.

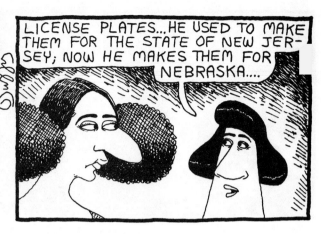

AL? ARE YOU OKAY? WHY ARE YOU SITTING IN THE CLOSET?

I'M WORKING UP TO DREAMING THE IMPOSSIBLE DREAM... WHEN I DO THAT, I'LL BE STANDING PROUDLY ON THE ROOF.

WHAT ARE YOU DOING NOW?

MULLING OVER THE IMPOSSIBLE DREAM.

I SEE.

WAS THAT FOREIGN OR DOMESTIC BEER?

I THINK MINE WAS FOREIGN OBJECT BEER!

YEP, LANCE, THERE'S NOTHING MORE RELAXING THAN A ROUND OF GOLF....

IF WE HAD A GOLF CART, I'D AGREE COMPLETELY.

MAYBE SOMEDAY.

FORE!!

NO NEED TO YELL.

OW!! — WHAT'S THE MATTER?

I JUST HIT MY ILIAC CREST ON THE EDGE OF THE SINK! OOH!!

ILIAC CREST?

IT'S PART OF THE PELVIC GIRDLE.

PELVIC GIRDLE?

NEVER MIND, LANCE—IT'S USELESS INFORMATION.

NOT IF YOU'RE A PELVIC GIRDLE SALESMAN.

TRUE.

WHAT'S ON THE AFTERNOON MOVIE, LANCE?

SOME WORLD WAR TWO EPIC CALLED "RETREAT, MY FOOT!"

SOUNDS LIKE A WINNER.

THIS OLD SERGEANT AND THESE YOUNG RECRUITS ARE DEFENDING THIS HILL, AND... WELL, LET'S JUST SAY THIS FILM BRIDGES THE GAP.

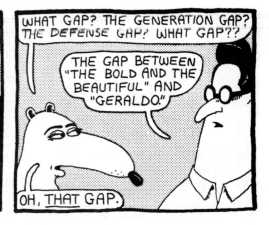

WHAT GAP? THE GENERATION GAP? THE DEFENSE GAP? WHAT GAP??

THE GAP BETWEEN "THE BOLD AND THE BEAUTIFUL" AND "GERALDO."

OH, THAT GAP.

THE GAG THAT WAS SO HILARIOUS, IT WAS PAINFUL TO BE INVOLVED IN IT...
"CLOSE-CAPTIONED FOR THE HERRING-IMPALED!"

HEH-HEH-HEH! HOY! HOY!

OOOH!

HA-HA-HA! OH, GOD!!

OH, HOW VERY RICH! HELP ME!!

HO-HO-HO! OH, MAN!!

A HEARTY FUSCO HANDCLASP TO OMAR DE QUASTA OF SHEBOYGAN FOR SENDING IN THIS JOKE, JUST BEFORE BEING RUSHED TO THE HOSPITAL! THANKS, GUY!!

Panel 1: HOW MANY TIMES HAVE I TOLD YOU NOT TO LEAVE YOUR THINGS ALL OVER THE FLOOR, AXEL?!!?

Panel 2: I THINK THE NUMBER IS IN THE LOW 400'S, RÖLF....

Panel 3: YOU WON'T GET VERY FAR WITH AN ATTITUDE LIKE THAT.

THAT YOU'VE TOLD ME 650-SOMETHING TIMES... DO YOU NEED THE EXACT FIGURE?

THAT WON'T BE NECESSARY.

Panel 4: DO YOU FEEL OKAY, RÖLF? YOU LOOK A LITTLE FUNNY.

IT'S NOTHING THAT NURSES AROUND THE CLOCK WOULDN'T CURE.

Panel 5: NURSES AROUND THE CLOCK?!?! ARE YOU THAT SICK???

Panel 6: I MAY BE RUNNING A SLIGHT TEMPERATURE, BUT OTHERWISE, AL, I FEEL FINE!

Panel 7: LANCE, WHILE YOU'RE UP, WOULD YOU DO ME A SMALL FAVOR?

I JUST DID YOU A FAVOR!

WHEN?

LATE MARCH...

EERIE TALES

Panel 8: I NEARLY BROKE MY NECK CHANGING THE LIGHT BULB IN THE CEILING FOR YOU!

Panel 9: WELL, NOW THAT IT'S CHANGED, AND YOU'RE STANDING RIGHT THERE, WOULD YOU MIND HITTING THE SWITCH? UNLESS YOU FIND THIS MISSION TOO DANGEROUS....

AXEL, THERE ARE TIMES WHEN I WOULD LOVE TO HIT THE SWITCH...

BUT PERHAPS CAPITAL PUNISHMENT IS A LITTLE SEVERE IN THIS CASE.

IS IT HOT IN HERE, GLORIA, OR IS IT ME?

BOTH, FURNACE MAN!

LET ME REPHRASE THAT...IS IT HUMID IN HERE, OR IS IT ME?

BOTH, WET BLANKET MAN FROM HELL!

THANK YOU, WILLARD SCOTT.

ART IS MY LIFE, AXEL...I GUESS THAT'S OBVIOUS JUST BY LOOKING AT MY WORK.

ART GARFUNKEL OR ART FLEMING?

ART LINKLETTER.

FROM PAIN OFTEN COMES ART...

OH, JEEZ!! GET IT OFF!!! PLEASE!!!

HMM..."WHEN AN EEL BITES YOUR LEG...

...AND THE PAIN MAKES YOU BEG...THAT'S A MORAY!" YEAH! I LIKE IT! GET ME A PENCIL, AXEL!

ANYTHING ELSE?

NAH.

117

121

WHAT ARE YOU DOING?

DISCOURAGING CROOKS...

NO RADIO IN CAR.

I REALIZE WE DO HAVE A RADIO IN THE CAR, BUT MAYBE IF THEY SEE THE SIGN THEY WON'T LOOK ANY FURTHER.

BUT LANCE, ISN'T THAT LYING?

IT'S LYING TO CROOKS, AL.

YOU KNOW WHAT THEY SAY ABOUT LYING...

THEY SAY YOU'LL BE LYING ON THE SIDEWALK IF YOU DON'T SHUT UP—ISN'T THAT WHAT THEY SAY?

CLOSE ENOUGH.

HOW ABOUT IF YOU DO THE DISHES FOR A CHANGE, LANCE?

WHAT DO I LOOK LIKE, GLORIA—

A GLUTTON FOR PUNISHMENT?

TAKE OUT THE PUNISHMENT PART, AND YOU MAY HAVE SOMETHING THERE....

AH, THE FLATTERY APPROACH.

IT COMES RIGHT BEFORE THE FRYING-PAN-OVER-THE-POMPADOUR APPROACH.

HOW VERY COLORFUL.

I'LL DO THE DISHES NEXT TIME, GLORIA, AS I DON'T RESPOND WELL TO THREATS...

LIKE I SAID, I'M NOT A GLUTTON FOR PUNISHMENT.

IT WOULD BE NICE IF YOU WERE A GLUTTON FOR JUSTICE, EQUALITY AND FAIR PLAY, LANCE.

PRETTY WORDS...VERY PATRICK HENRY...WELL, I SAY GIVE ME LIBERTY, OR GIVE ME A BREAK.

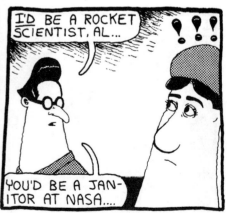

THE
END